WHAT RIMBAUD SAID
AFTER THE AMPUTATION

WHAT RIMBAUD SAID
AFTER THE AMPUTATION

CAVEH ZAHEDI

Sticking Place Books
2025

ISBN 979-8-89976-031-0

CONTENTS

Introduction

INTRODUCTION

My favorite poet is Wallace Stevens and his influence, I feel, is absurdly obvious in these pages. The great literary critic Harold Bloom speaks exhaustively of "the anxiety of influence" that any writer feels towards a previous writer whose work has meant a lot to him or her, and he points out that Stevens himself was deeply influenced by Walt Whitman. Harold Bloom makes the case that a great poet tries, in the words of Wallace Stevens:

> ...to drive away
> The shadow of his fellows from the skies,
> And, from their stale intelligence released,
> To make a new intelligence prevail?

Well, I would never call Wallace Stevens' intelligence stale, but I suppose it could be argued that imitations of anyone are stale, the way the paintings of someone imitating Van Gogh or Picasso or Andy Warhol would inevitably be experienced as derivative and stale. In fact, I would argue that 90% of the art I see in galleries feels derivative and stale. To quote the artist Robert Henri, "We are not here to do what has already been done," and yet that seems to be what most so-called artists are doing.

Another of my favorite poets is John Ashbery, who strikes me as radically original, despite Harold Bloom's thoughtful excavation of Ashbery's profound debt to both Wallace Stevens and Walt Whitman. But it's almost impossible for me, with rare exceptions, to detect the influence of either Wallace Stevens or Walt Whitman in Ashbery's work. For Bloom, that's what makes Ashbery what he would call a "strong" poet.

In his 1920 book *The Sacred Wood*, T. S. Eliot famously wrote: "Immature poets imitate; mature poets steal; bad poets deface what they take, and good poets make it into something better, or at least different." I would never claim that it's even possible to make "something better" than Wallace Stevens. That's like claiming that it's possible to make a better God than God. But hopefully it's possible to make something "at least different."

I've never thought particularly highly of the poems I've occasionally written, mostly because they struck me as overly influenced by Stevens. One of them, "Thirteen Ways of Looking at the Idaho Moon," is arguably closer to a pastiche. But reading them again, with the distance of several years after their composition, I am struck by how different they are from Stevens' magisterial style.

Part of the reason for that is that there are additional influences at play. The two that strike me most forcefully upon re-reading these poems are Rimbaud and Basho. Their influence inflects that of Stevens to produce something that is, hopefully, "at least different." Surely, there is some fourth thing, which I guess is my own consciousness, reading and mis-reading those singular writers.

All this is just to say that I have been persuaded to publish these poems in part because their immense debt to Stevens no longer strikes me as embarrassingly obvious. The influence is palpable, but I am hopefully not merely defacing what I take and, despite the blatant stealing, the money laundering operation that this book of poems represents somehow manages to evade detection by the relevant law enforcement agencies.

I hesitate to even call these scattered jottings "poems." But I don't know what else to call them. I would urge you to put this down and read Wallace Stevens, or Rimbaud, or Basho instead. I promise you it would be a much better use of your time. But if you insist on reading further, I just want to say that anything good in these pages was probably stolen from one of them, and anything bad is me being caught shop-lifting.

To quote Stevens one more time, writing about his own poems (this is from "The Planet on the Table"):

> It was not important that they survive.
> What mattered was that they should bear
> Some lineament or character,
>
> Some affluence, if only half-perceived,
> In the poverty of their words,
> Of the planet of which they were part.

I hope these poems, despite the poverty of their words (and of my consciousness), nevertheless bear some lineament or character, if only half-perceived, not only of the planet of which they were part but also of the epoch of which they are no longer part,

Venice Beach, 1997

ABRACADABRA

When Ali Baba found the secret word
That unlocked the cave with all its treasures,
He wanted to write it down
So as to be able to repeat at will its elusive pleasures.

But the word was twenty-four years long
And Ali Baba died before he could get it all down.
And so the word was lost
And the leaves of his diary turned brown.

And then, on September 14, 1974,
A miracle occurred.
The word was made flesh
And a gift conferred.

But it was still a very long word
And twenty-four more years had to pass,
Until on September 14, 1998,
That gift could be received at last.

Washington DC, 1961

ALCHEMICANA

The alchemical broth
Is stirred and stirred
Until the precipitate clots
Into the magic word.

San Francisco, 1999

AND WHAT IF EVERYTHING WERE PERFECT

Hansel did not like what he saw.
This place was ugly
And harsh
And he missed his ma.

Gretel regretted having come this far.
She was hungry
And lost
And ready to say au revoir.

Just then the wicked witch showed up
And invited them to sup.

Hansel and Gretel had read the book
And feared the food would kill them.
But they were famished
And so partook.

And the spell was broken.
And then

Hansel and Gretel saw
That this place wasn't what it seemed
And they fell down on their knees
In awe.

San Francisco, 2003

ANGELIC GANG

I
I am a prisoner
In an angelic gang.
I break this rock
Into yin and yang.

II
There is an angelic gang
And a host.
They play their harps.
They propose a toast.

Valentine's Day, 2001

San Francisco, 2001

ART HISTORY

I remember when you slept
On my bed
While I read
On the couch and I kept
Looking at you
And wishing I drew.

San Francisco, 2003

AT THE ARITHMETICAL CENTER OF LIFE

In the Book of Life
In which your name is written,
In a handwriting that is not your own,
Two dates are writ in stone.

One I recognize
As the numerical symbol
Of everything I love.
It is, for me,
The password and the key
To Heaven and to Love.

The other is illegible to me.
It is a date I have never seen,
And dread.
It is the numerical symbol of everything I fear:
The password and the key
To the Mathematics of the Dead.

I will live my life
In the interval between
These numbers,
And I will die serene.
For my days have already
Been counted.
And the number of my days
Is the same
As yours.

Brittany, 1972

THE BOOKS ON THE CHAIR

The books on the chair
Are just there.
They don't mean a thing.
They simply ring
With their own this-ness.
They mind their own business.
So there.

Austin, 2004

CAN'T WRITE NOW

Time to go and see the sky
Before it passes irrevocably by.

Rome, 2007

CHRISTMAS ALREADY

Christmas already!
Arriving empty-handed
With only this haiku.

Paris, 1985

DANS UN NOUVEL APPARTEMENT À PARIS

Dans un nouvel appartement
À Paris,
Néo-gothique avec un dongeon
Qu'elle meubla soigneusement,
Un yacht tout blanc les menait.

Et il y mourut en 1956
Après la revolution.

C'est sous cette forme
Qu'ils devaient remonter
Les tristesses de l'epoque.

✒   ✒   ✒

In a new apartment in Paris,
Neo-gothic with a dungeon,
That she decorated with care
A bright white yacht carried them along.

And he died there in 1956
After the revolution.

It was in this form
That they had to traverse
The sadnesses of the epoch.

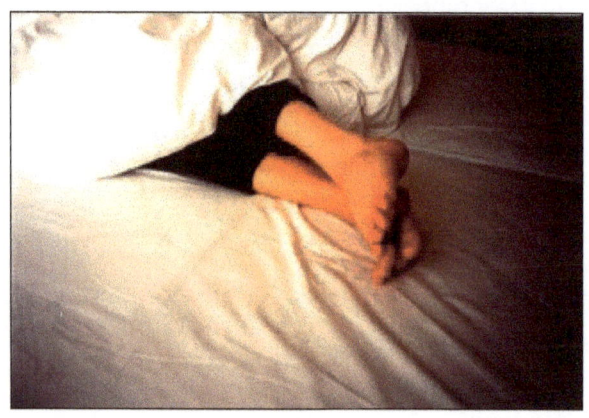

Munich, 1991

DEAF AND DUMB

You will never know
The unutterable joy
Of sleeping next to you.

Grand Canyon, 1967

DODGE DART SWINGER

There is a car
On an empty road
Late at night.

Venice Beach, 1997

DUDLEY DO-RIGHT

At forty-four, Dudley Do-Right
Moved into an attic apartment
In Venice in order to be
By the beach. There was no way to
Write to him other than by using
His new address.

New address: 44 Dudley Ave, Apt. B,
Venice, CA 90291

Plenty of Sand

New phone/fax: (310) 399-8901

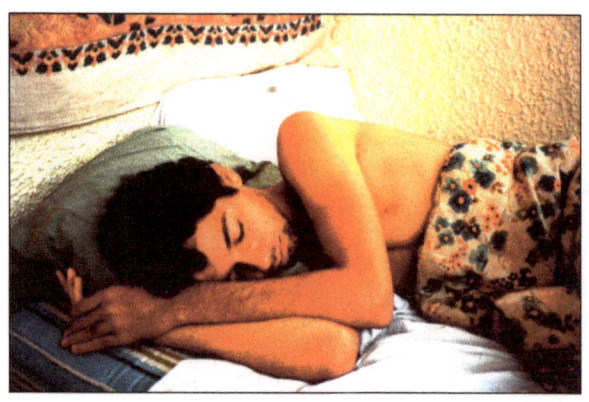

Berkeley, 1983

EPITAPH

This was what he had wanted:
To lie in the sun with never a care,
To feel that his body was air
And his skin unhaunted.

Seattle, 1999

FAVORITE POETS

1) Wallace Stevens
2) Rimbaud
3) Basho
4) John Ashbery
5) Rumi
6) T. S. Eliot
7) Stéphane Mallarmé
8) Gerard Manley Hopkins
9) Francis Ponge
10) Emily Dickinson

Other Poets I like
Hart Crane
Paul Verlaine
William Butler Yeats
René Char
Percy Bysshe Shelley
Rainer Maria Rilke
John Donne
William Shakespeare
Dylan Thomas
Germain Nouveau

Venice Beach, 1997

FIRST DAY OF SPRING, 1998

A day like any other, really.
Except for that extra half-second of noticing.
The sun declines and I wish it wouldn't.
I wish it would stop.
I wish it would wait for me.
But it is waiting,
It always has, and it always will.

Solar deity, ever-careening towards me,
Inviting and inviting.
And once a year, for an instant,
I accept the invitation.
And then decline it again.

It is a dance notation we are both devising
As we rush headlong into
God.

Corsica, 1972

THE GENIE IN THE BOTTLE

I love you but
We are not alone here.
God is here too.

And I can only kiss you
Over and over again,
Knowing that I am getting no further in my quest to
    become one with you,
Except by the slow attrition
Of my naive strategies for salvation.

And now I crumble to the ground
And have no will to rise again.
I hate myself and long
For the round of seasons
To break me beneath its wheel
And pinion. And when the final brakeshaft
    is released
And I go hurtling
Into space,
I will not regret the rack and steering
That brought me to my knees
When I tried
To kiss your face.

These are the things that I have seen.
I will forget them soon
And they will leave no trace
Except for the lines on every face
I happen to espy
As I walk by.

I love and I love the slow decline
Of feelings sliding in and out of fine,
Of memories that are torn apart by time
And then stitched back together
    on the sewing machine of rhyme.

I wonder and I wonder how to think
About the brink on which I totter,
Like an otter about to sink
Into the rushing waters
Of time.

And then another day comes.
The face in the mirror is not the same.
The space in the calendar has shifted its domain
And we are no longer who we were.

The final piece of the puzzle will come
Tumbling from the sky
When the lover's eye
Is indistinguishable from the eye of Satan or of God,
And time ceases to be the corrosive rust
On the pelvic thrust between
You and I.

And yet there is a voice that does not falter,
A face that smiles upon us from every altar
And which we then destroy like children
Delighting in our power to deface
The indecipherable letters we sometimes trace
Unknowing in the air,
Not knowing that every gesture is a prayer
And that every prayer always comes true,
Or that the genie in the bottle is always you.

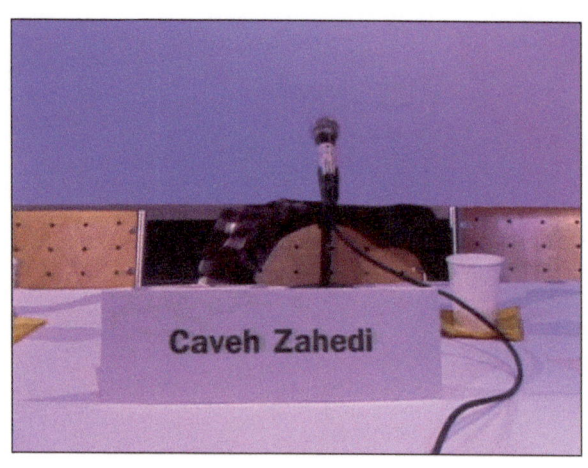

Chicago, 2002

THE GIFT OF GAB

The gift of gab.
The gift of goo.
The gift of gobbledy gook.

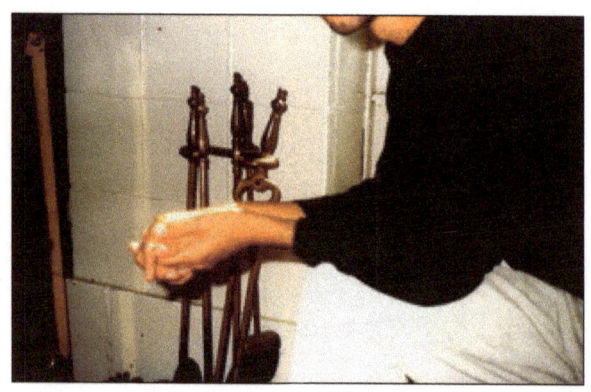

Los Angeles, 1983

THE HAND OF GOD

He wanted to write her a poem,
But he was afraid.
He wanted to tell her he loved her,
And to look into her eyes without preconception or
    a mask of any kind,

But he was afraid.
He wanted to kiss her over and over again,
Or just once for a period longer than he had ever
    dared to kiss before,
But he was too afraid.

Instead, he went limpingly about his life,
Only half-conscious of the eternal and ever-self-
    renewing miracle
That was being born at each and every moment right
    beside him.
But he could apprehend its presence every time he
    stopped

And dared to open his eyes for even a split second.
And he could see that all of the prophecies had
    actually come true,
And that the second coming was already at hand.
And he held her hand,
And he knew that it was the hand of God.
And he was afraid.

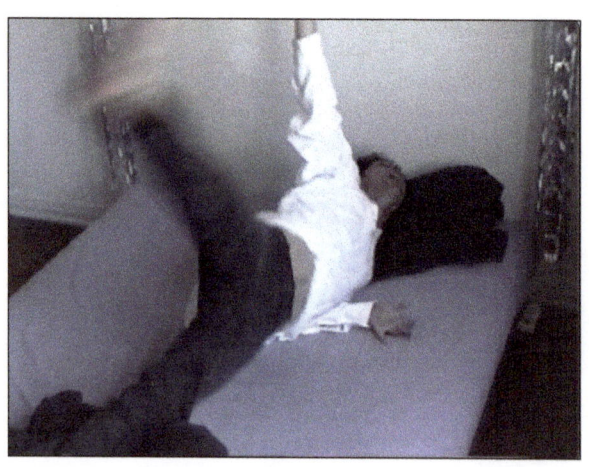

Santa Monica, 1996

HAPPY BIRTHDAY

Another year
Like a bullet from a gun.
That deer is dead.
Let us now eat venison.

San Francisco, 2003

THE HERO HAS AMNESIA

I
Sometimes he forgot why he had come to this castle,
or that the witch asleep in the other room was actu-
ally a beautiful princess who had been put under a
spell.

II
And then sometimes he remembered in a flash that
he had seen this place before, in a dream or in a
picture in a book.

III
But mostly he was haunted by imaginary dragons
whom he hacked and flailed at, half-hallucinating.

IV
The castle was dirty. The witch was ugly. The fight
against the dragons bloody. But something within
him knew that there was something he had come to
do.

V
He saw it clearly once or twice. And he also saw
how it would end. The witch would be transformed.
The dragons would disappear. And the castle would
be clean again.

VI

But for now he was condemned to hack and flail and recite once more the indecipherable incantation until, in a harmony of parts, the sideshow to which they had been condemned would end and the true performance begin at last.

San Francisco, 2004

LAST NIGHT AFTER WORK

Last night I watched your face
As you spoke to me
About your evening.

I loved and understood each instant
Of its perpetually changing surface
Like a light box affected by sound.

I could go on and on about each expression
And what it means.
I could go on and on about how much I love each one
Because I understand what it means.

I have never known anyone before.
It is like meeting God.

Rotterdam, 2005

THE LIFE AND DECHT
OF BERTOLT BRECHT

Brecht was a lot more fun than you'd expect -
The "alienation" only a façade
Like a stage set.
The papier-mâché of our expectations crumbles,
Worn down by the beating sands of this hour glass
From which we try, absurdly, to drink,
This snow globe lifted by a child's hand and shaken,
To see what falls and what remains.

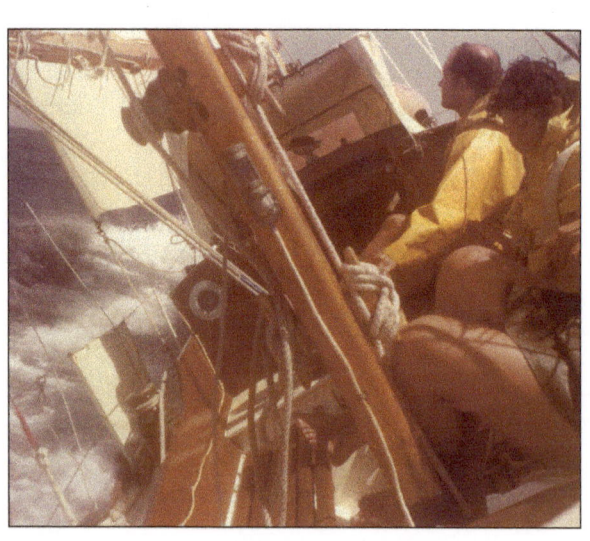

Corsica, 1973

LOST AT SEA

I
Lawrence Welk knew what it meant
To play a polka and really mean it
On the waxed dance floors
Of empty ballrooms filled to bursting
With soap bubbles bursting
For television cameras bursting
With period optimism.

He always thought of himself as a modern-day saint,
The poor man's Chopin,
Poised to absolve all absent-minded septagenarians
In the hullaballoo
Of his immortal instrument,
And in the to and fro
Of dance steps undertaken
By undertakers and their spouses
At undertaker conventions across the land.

The land remains.
The undertakers have died,
But the undertakers are buried in the land
While Lawrence Welk is lost at sea.

II
We too swim in that sea,
Clinging to life vests made of ether,
Watching the lifeboats perpetually sinking
On the horizon's edge,
In the time before Columbus was born.
This is the period
Of our resubstantiation
In the conviviality
Of a pleasure cruise,
And in the transubstantiation
Of an ocean liner's orchestra
Playing "The Sinking of the Titanic"
As we all fall down
Into the eternal waters
Of consubstantiation.

III
And so we sleep
Until the scattered nightmares that still haunt
Awaken us as is their wont
And we rise up from the deep

And we stretch our limbs
And we sing hymns
To Him who is not He nor She
But We.

Boise, 1989

MAP OF OREGON GOES HERE

He believed in fate,
And it was in that state
That he had found and lost
His faith.

Los Angeles, 1997

THE MOSLEM IN ME

The Moslem in me
Gets down on one knee,
Lowers my head to the ground
And His dark doctrines propounds.

Chicago, 1984

THE MUSIC OF WINTER

Here none but me see you
Fingering the music of winter
And watching the fall go by
Beneath the milk and honey sky
Of summer's flood.

Corsica, 1972

NO MATTER

Whether I sink or swim
In the plethora of this place,
Space has shattered
And matter is pleased.
I cease and I desist.
I am deceased
And no longer exist,
And easily the mind swims
In perfect peace or sinks
In this bliss.

Munich, 1991

OF D'S TRAGIC GRANDEUR

I
Who could describe
The incomparable mix
Of sadness and of bliss
In her voice
And in her eyes?
Who could describe?

II
Who could say
Why she moved that way,
The tragic grandeur
In her bones,
The temporality of stones?
Who could say?

III
Who could see
The infinity within,
The exaltation in the skin?
Who could see?

Me.

Rome, 2008

OPEN SESAME

Open,
Heart.
Please open.

Austin, 1991

PERIWINKLE

I can't wait till today.

Kauai, 1994

PHOTOGRAPH OF A GIRAFFE

I
Among the giraffes you know
Is one with vertigo.

II
Was it a mutation?
A compensation for a fall?
No tree is that tall.

III
A neck like an arm.
A head like a hand.
I don't understand.

Santa Monica, 1995

THE STIGMATA

When the stigmata first appeared,
I was scared.
It was just too weird.
But I'm used to it now.

Corsica, 1974

STUPID ME

Stupid me
Who cannot see
The sea.

If love existed,
And it does,
I would not fear
The loss of hair.

If love existed,
And it does,
I would not fear you
As I do.

Rome, 2007

A SYLVIA BEACH OF THE MIND

If there is a beach
Beyond our reach
(And there is),
A shore
Beyond this mortal portal
(Such a door exists),
And if that place is bliss
(And it is),
Then my most fervent wish
Is to attain that state
Sooner rather than late.

Los Angeles, 1992

THERE IS A HILL

There is a hill in my neighborhood
That I climb and descend each day
(It is slowly eroding).
But in my heart there is a pit
Whose depths I have never plumbed
(That's why my heart is corroding).

Paris, 1985

THERE IS A RIVER

I
There is a river and I know it flows,
But God knows where it goes.

II
The river runs hither and dither,
But the flowers by the river wither.

III
The river rises when it rains,
But the river also flows inside my veins.

IV
The insects watch the river seep into the plain.
They see and understand beneath the pouring rain.

V
The river in my dream
Seemed more real than this stupid stream.

VI
River, river on the plain,
The waters of my heart make me insane.

VII
The river is green or brown,
But the sea-queen wears a sea-weed crown.

VIII
The river has a bed.
In it I will rest my head.

IX
There is a river in hell.
I'm going there. Farewell.

Berkeley, 1983

THIRTEEN WAYS OF LOOKING AT THE IDAHO MOON

I
No moon.
Why is the sky so bright?

II
The stars are shards,
Reflecting the moon.

III
Lovers speak of the moon.
Of whom does the moon speak?

IV
Because the moon is sad,
I am sad.
Because the moon is sad,
I am less sad.

V
When the moon is full,
People say it's only a phase.

VI
They speak of the hornéd moon.
They spoke of it before I was born.

VII
The milky way
Is moon milk.

VIII
The moon is not a womb.
The moon is a stone.
May I die beneath it.

IX
I used to hate the moon.
I used to hate myself.

X
The man in the moon is dead.
The moon smiles
Because the moon remembers
When they wed.

XI
One night, I saw the world on fire.
All the firemen in the world folded their arms.
It was only the moon,
Rising.

XII
Everyday,
The tide tries to run away.
But it can't.

XIII
I have never seen the moon,
And I never will.
And yet, this love.

San Francisco, 2003

THIS IS BLISS

When she kissed him,
That was bliss.
She no longer kisses him now.
This, too, is bliss.

San Francisco, 2007

THIS SCHISM

God dictates,
And I listen
To his catechism.

Fontainebleau, 1973

WANTING TO SAY THANK YOU, THANK YOU, THANK YOU

I
That would be the utmost embrace:
To move unhurriedly through space,
To feel the simple air
Wrap its arms around one's face.

II
That would be to hold hands:
To run fingers through the sand
To find a bone,
To pick up a stone
Or to put it down
Or just to leave it where it was.

III
That would be giving birth:
To be buried by children in the earth,
To hear in the quietest drum of the ear
The ecstatic call of an alien hum.

Los Angeles, 1991

WEEKEND AT THE BEACH

Saturday

The sea today was gray
And tinged with haze.
The waves that slithered in succession on the sand
Spelled out a phrase
Which I could sense
But could not understand.

Sunday

The sea today
Was not a color that I have ever seen.
It was alive
And frightened me.
And I turned away.

Savigny-sur-Orge, 1973

WHAT RIMBAUD SAID
AFTER THE AMPUTATION

If I'd have known you gun men were comin'
I'd have saved my money.

Honolulu, 1994

THE WINDS OF FATE

The winds of fate:
They blow me here,
They blow me there.
They blow me here.

I would like to thank Lee Ritchie for encouraging me to publish these poems and for his preternatural editing acumen, Paul Cronin for his borderline psychotic open-mindedness in being willing to publish this book, Adelaide Faith for being unimaginably wonderful and for her kind blurb, and my exes for whom many of these poems were written in lieu of flowers on Valentine's Day.